Author's Note

The object of this book is to introduce the reader to the life and work of the greatest playwright in the English language, William Shakespeare. It does so by telling the story of the writing and production of *Macbeth*, one of his best-known plays.

This is not a straightforward task. We know very few personal details about Shakespeare and there are also wide gaps in our knowledge about the theatre of his time and the way his plays were first performed. To overcome this, I have done two things. Wherever possible, I have based the story on facts and figures supported by historical evidence. For example, all the information about the Globe theatre is verifiable, as is the performance of *Macbeth* before Kings James and Christian at Hampton Court in August 1606. Where there are gaps in our knowledge, to give the book colour and interest I have added plausible detail of my own. Although there is nothing to tell us that Shakespeare went to the Boar's Head to tell the King's Men about his plans for a play based on the reign of King Macbeth, there is nothing to suggest he might not have done so. Similarly, we do not know for sure that King Christian was drunk during the performance of *Macbeth*, but as he was well-known for his heavy drinking, it is a fair conjecture. At no point have I strayed into pure fantasy. All the information in this book is either fact, or as close to fact as we can come.

Stewart Ross

For Ella, Jake and Leo Reading
S.R.

For my mother
T.K.

Text copyright © 1994 Stewart Ross
Illustrations copyright © 1994 Tony Karpinski
Additional illustrations copyright © 1994 Victor Ambrus

Black and white drawing on endpapers and pages 7 and 19: *Study for the Long View of London from Bankside*, by Wenceslaus Hollar (1607 – 1677). Reproduced with the permission of the Yale Center for British Art, Paul Mellon Collection.

BRITISH LIBRARY CATALOGUING IN PUBLICATION DATA
A catalogue record for this book is available from the British Library.

ISBN 1 85602 114 9

First published in 1994 by
David Bennett Books Ltd
94 Victoria Street
St Albans
Herts AL1 3TG

Consultants:
Professor Andrew Gurr
Professor Stanley Wells

Typesetting by Turner Typesetting
Production by Imago
Manufactured in China

SHAKESPEARE AND MACBETH
The story behind the play

STEWART ROSS

Illustrated by
TONY KARPINSKI
and
VICTOR AMBRUS

Foreword by
KENNETH BRANAGH

DAVID BENNETT BOOKS

Foreword
by Kenneth Branagh

The first I ever heard of William Shakespeare, was when famous phrases or lines from his plays would appear on TV or in films, usually spoken by the great actor Laurence Olivier. Prince Hamlet's famous words 'To be or not to be' I first heard in a TV advert for cigars!

A few years later, it was my turn to be taught Shakespeare 'officially' at school. We had to read *The Merchant of Venice*. Each of us had to speak a section of it aloud to the rest of the class. The language was very unfamiliar and difficult and I didn't understand a word of it. All I knew was that Shakespeare was a world famous English playwright, lived around 400 years ago and was *supposed* to be brilliant.

It wasn't until I saw one of his plays performed by actors that I knew what my teachers meant. The play was *Romeo and Juliet*, the famous love story about a young boy and girl, each from warring families, who fall in love. They hope that their marriage might bring an end to their families' feud. I was fourteen and recognised many things in the story — people from different backgrounds having forbidden relationships, and the gang warfare. It was a very exciting, emotional tale. There were fights and surprisingly, lots of humour. The human situations seemed so real and familiar that the language seemed absolutely natural.

My experience at the theatre was very different from reading the plays 'cold' in class. Also, many of the books about Shakespeare's life seemed terribly stuffy.

This book is far from stuffy. It conveys much of the excitement I felt when I was first introduced to 'live' Shakespeare. It concentrates on how Shakespeare came to write one of his most famous plays, *Macbeth*. This is a very bloodthirsty tale of how a famous Scottish warrior was tempted by witches to follow his darkest ambitions. In fulfilling them he kills a king and very nearly goes mad. His wife really does go mad and both their lives end violently.

There is also a great deal of information in this book about Shakespeare's life and the fascinating period in which he lived. The book shows Shakespeare as a very charismatic man who wrote marvellous stories that people of all ages can identify with. If you enjoy reading this, I hope you'll have the opportunity to see one of his plays on stage or screen. I think you'll find it worthwhile – and fun.

Enjoy!

Kenneth Branagh

1605

London. A chaotic sprawling city, by far the biggest in the British Isles and fast becoming one of the largest in Europe. It has spread far beyond its medieval walls and moved into the surrounding countryside, swallowing up farms and villages.

Church spires and the stone buildings of the mighty overlook wooden houses set in a maze of winding streets. To the west lie the great cathedral and the palace of Westminster; to the east the massive bulk of the Tower of London stands sentinel beside crowded wharves and jetties. And in the heart of the ancient city, St Paul's rises like a great rock amid a sea of tiled and thatched roofs.

A single bridge spans the river. On the muddy southern bank, among the brothels and bearbaiting arenas and only a few steps from open fields, a new construction has recently appeared: a huge, many-sided building with a small, domed tower – the Globe theatre. Here a group of actors, the King's Men, perform their plays.

The New Play

It's a grey overcast afternoon in late September. The King's Men are nearing the end of a performance of *Hamlet*, the last in their summer season of plays. *Hamlet* lasts several hours and is performed without a break. The groundlings – poorer people watching the play in the open air – are becoming restless. One man, who is clearly the worse for drink, yells at the actors to hurry up. Annoyed by the disturbance, the men and women sitting in the covered galleries shout back at the troublemaker, telling him to keep quiet.

A buzz of conversation goes round the theatre, making it difficult for the actors to concentrate. The boy playing Hamlet's mother momentarily forgets his lines, and for a minute or two it looks as though the performance may grind to a halt. But attendants haul out the drunkard, and the show goes on.

By five o'clock it has grown even more gloomy, and begins to rain. Many of the groundlings leave. The rest of the audience pull their cloaks tightly around them and strain to catch the actors' words above the noise of the downpour. Stage hands bring flaming torches to throw more light on the stage, watching anxiously for sparks that might set the wooden theatre alight.

At the end of the performance, the applause does not last long, as the playgoers are keen to return to the city before nightfall. After a few bows the actors troop backstage to the tiring house to change. A few minutes later the torches are extinguished and gloom descends on the empty theatre.

Empty? Not quite. A balding, middle-aged man wrapped in a heavy cloak remains in his seat. Lost in his thoughts, he sits gazing at the darkening stage.

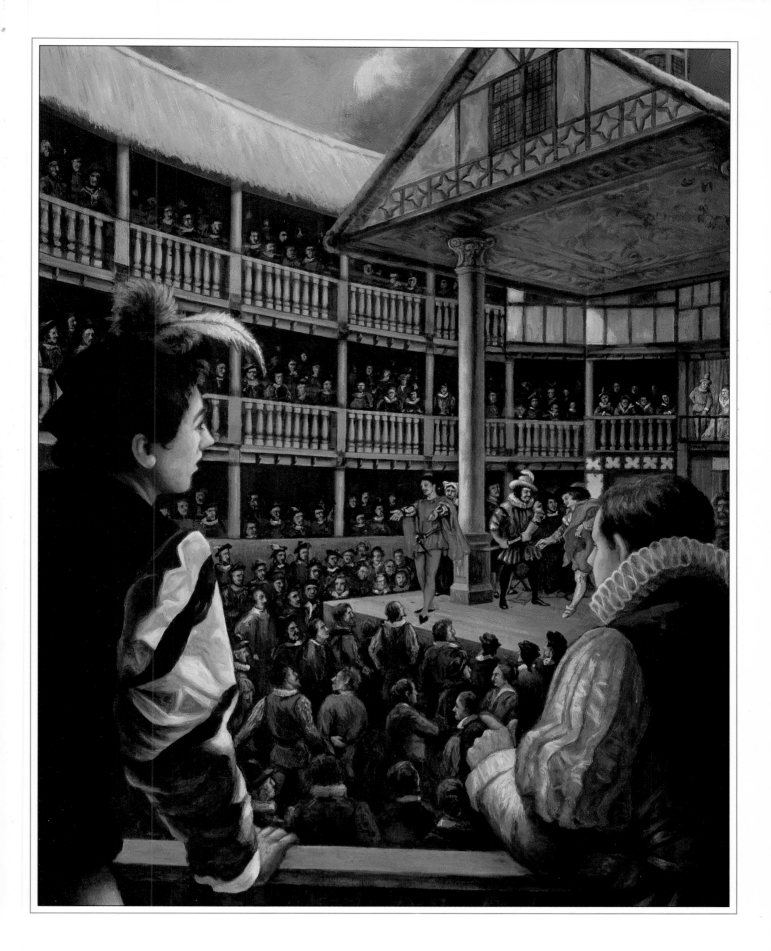

IX
NINE

Meanwhile, in the dimly-lit tiring house, the actors chat about the performance as they take off their rich gowns and dresses. The young lad who stumbled over his lines apologises to the rest of the cast. The others commiserate with him, and grumble among themselves about the behaviour of the groundlings.

The company are looking forward to indoor winter performances at court or in the houses of the aristocracy. Such patrons pay handsomely, and although they do not always give the drama as much attention as the actors would like, they are not in the habit of interrupting.

As well as a number of Shakespearian favourites – *Hamlet, Romeo and Juliet, The Merry Wives of Windsor, Henry V* and his latest, *King Lear* – they have been asked to stage *The Fair Maid of Bristow,* and Ben Jonson's *Every Man in his Humour.* It's hard work being one of the King's Players, taking a different part every day.

Richard Burbage, who has been playing Hamlet, suggests that it's about time Shakespeare

wrote a new play for their repertoire. The others groan. Another play means more rehearsal and yet more lines to learn. It's all very well for Burbage, they complain – he gets all the best parts. Someone quips that all Burbage wants is another opportunity to show off in front of an audience.

The door of the tiring house opens and the cloaked figure from the auditorium enters the room. It is William Shakespeare, who has just arrived back from a visit to his wife and family in Stratford-upon-Avon.

Shakespeare is a popular man. The cast gather round him, asking him what he thought of the performance. He says it was excellent, although he could have done without the drunkard's interruption.

After a few minutes' talk, Shakespeare suggests that he and the principal members of the company take a ferry across the river to an inn, to talk over an idea he has for a new play.

Burbage smiles. Without a word, he gathers up his cloak and follows Shakespeare and half a dozen actors out into the rain.

An hour later, the players are sitting round a table in an upstairs room at the Boar's Head in East Cheap. A fire is blazing on the hearth, and they are drinking freely, filling their glasses from a large jug of wine.

Shakespeare proposes to write a play which will appeal specifically to King James. The king is keen on the theatre, and at his accession in 1603 he became personal patron of the company. As a result, they changed their name from the Lord Chamberlain's Men to the King's Men. Aware of how important it is to keep in with James, the others accept Shakespeare's suggestion.

But when they hear that he is thinking of a play about Scotland, there is a chorus of protest. Like most seventeenth-century English people, they are full of prejudice against Scotland, even though their king is Scottish. They imagine it to be a cold, wet, dreary country inhabited by barbarians, who have flocked south since the beginning of James's reign to feed like leeches off England's riches.

Shakespeare has strong arguments for a Scottish setting. He reminds his friends that plays set in Scotland have recently met with success on the English stage. He then quietly points out that whatever their private views about Scotland and its inhabitants, it is James's native land. After some discussion, his colleagues are convinced.

Shakespeare reveals that he is planning to write about Macbeth, who ruled Scotland between 1040 and 1057. The story is quite well known, and he believes it will make an excellent drama.

This is the story of Macbeth that Shakespeare gathered from his researches into 11th-century Scottish history. Macbeth was an army commander held in high trust by King Duncan of Scotland. On a journey to Forres he met with three witches who prophesied that Macbeth would become king of Scotland. The prophecy fanned Macbeth's ambition, and led him to murder Duncan. Duncan's sons, Malcolm and Donalbain, fled the country, and Macbeth became king. At first he ruled well, but he soon turned into a terrible tyrant. In the seventeenth year of his reign, Duncan's son Malcolm raised an army in England, and invaded Scotland. His army defeated Macbeth's, and Macbeth was killed in the battle.

Shakespeare is a busy man. As well as writing plays and acting in minor roles, he is also one of the Company's sharers, or shareholders. This group of about ten actor-businessmen owns the theatre and finds the money for staging performances. Costs include paying for plays to be copied out, buying costumes and props, and paying the other actors. In return, they share the profits – perhaps as much as £50 in a good month.

Shakespeare's primary task, therefore, is to see that the company makes money. That means writing plays with broad popular appeal. There is no point in producing the most brilliant intellectual masterpiece if it is performed to an empty theatre.

With so much on his hands, it is not easy for him to find time to sit down and write a new play. Shakespeare researches his subject over the winter of 1605–6. By the spring, with the company anxious to start rehearsals, he is finally ready to begin writing.

Shakespeare's education at Stratford-upon-Avon grammar school gave him a strong background in Latin and classical mythology, but he learned very little British history. He therefore relies heavily on one of the most up-to-date and popular history books of his day – Holinshed's *Chronicles of England, Scotland and Ireland*. He has already successfully adapted stories from the English *Chronicles* for some of his earlier plays, such as *Henry IV* (in two parts) and *Henry V*. Now he turns to the Scottish *Chronicles* for the story of Macbeth.

However, before long he decides that Holinshed's version of events is not quite what he is looking for. What he has in mind is not a history play, but a dramatic tragedy, where time and place are less important than the characters and the action. So he combines two of Holinshed's stories (the reign of King Macbeth, and the murder of King Duff by Donwald and his wife), altering both to suit his needs.

These are some of the changes Shakespeare makes:

◆ He compresses all the events of Macbeth's seventeen-year reign into less than a year, and omits his considerable achievements.

◆ In the *Chronicles*, Macbeth's friend Banquo takes part in Duncan's murder. But Banquo is thought to be King James's ancestor, so Shakespeare makes him into an innocent, noble man.

◆ King Duncan is changed from a feeble young man into an old and respected ruler at the end of a long and successful reign.

◆ King James believed in witches, and wrote a book on witchcraft, so the emphasis on witches is increased, and Shakespeare introduces a ghost into the story.

◆ He also adds references to events of the early part of James's reign, such as the trial of Father Garnet, a Roman Catholic priest who was executed in 1606 for allegedly being involved in the Gunpowder Plot.

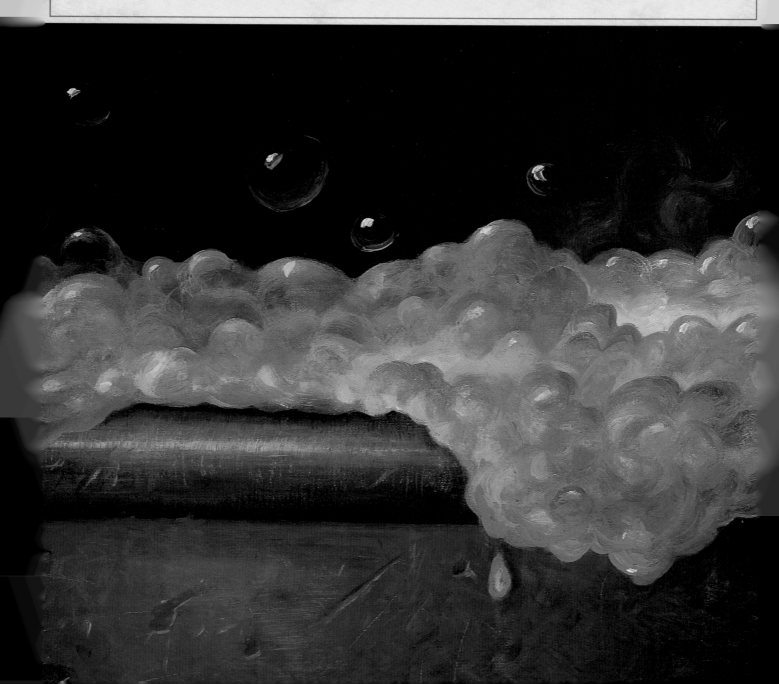

There are no female actors in Shakespeare's time. It is considered immoral for women to appear on a public stage. All female roles are played by boys, usually in their early teens.

Macbeth is written almost entirely in verse. This is normal at the time for this type of play. It is also a good way to make the profound speeches of the central characters more memorable. But for the speech of the ordinary characters, Shakespeare generally uses prose. In this way, he can let the audience know what type of character is speaking.

XVIII
EIGHTEEN

The changes increase the story's drama and make it more appealing to Shakespeare's audience, particularly the King. Shakespeare focuses the story sharply around Macbeth and his wife: their characters are central to the play.

Once he has a rough idea of the plot and main characters in his mind, Shakespeare divides the play into five acts, each with a number of scenes. Knowing King James to be impatient, he makes sure that *Macbeth* will be a short play. He also tries to write characters which suit the actors of the King's Men. For example, he knows he can write a good part for Lady Macbeth, because the company includes a boy who is excellent at playing women.

Finally, Shakespeare has to bear in mind the size, design and shape of the theatres in which *Macbeth* is likely to be performed. The most important of these is the Globe.

The Globe

The Globe theatre was built in early 1599, on boggy ground on the south bank of the Thames. When new, the Globe was the finest theatre in the country. But it burned down in July 1613 during a performance of Shakespeare's *Henry VIII,* when sparks from a cannon set fire to the thatch.

Construction
Wood and thatch on
brick foundations.

Shape
A polygon (actually thought to
have had 20 sides).

Approximate size
Overall diameter 30 m.
Height, 12 m to top of galleries,
20 m to top of 'Heavens' (the
roof over the stage).
Yard, 21 m diameter.
Stage, 10-12 m wide.

Estimated capacity
Approximately 3,000, with 1,500
standing in the yard around the
stage. Two narrow entrances,
each admitting only one
person at a time.

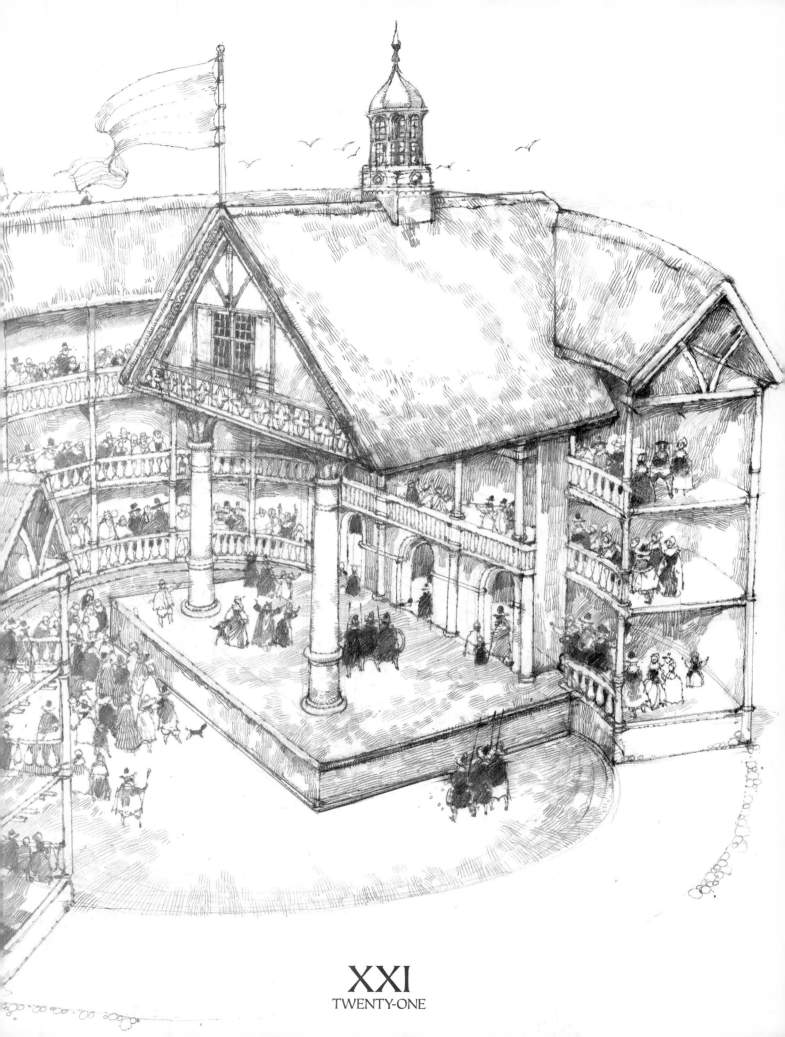

XXI
TWENTY-ONE

1606

M ay. It is a frantic time of year for all companies of actors, but especially for the King's Men, who have a reputation to live up to. They have about thirty plays to get ready for the coming season. They have performed most of them before, but several, including *Macbeth,* have to be staged from scratch.

As soon as Shakespeare finishes the manuscript, he shows the play to his fellow sharers. Once he has their approval, he arranges for individual parts to be copied out by a scribe. This saves the expense of copying the whole play out for each actor, and prevents the complete text from falling into the hands of rival companies.

The parts are now ready and with the cast. Some actors have already learned their lines, others are holding up proceedings by rehearsing with scripts in their hands.

Shakespeare is living near the theatre in Southwark. He spends all his time at the Globe, rehearsing parts that he is playing himself, offering advice on other productions and taking special care to see that *Macbeth* is performed just as he wishes it to be.

The company are relieved to find that *Macbeth* is easy to stage. Unlike some of Shakespeare's plays, it does not require any complicated special effects.

Scarcely more than three weeks after Shakespeare has finished writing the play, it is ready for its first performance. Some lines were even changed during rehearsal. It is not as well prepared

as he would like it to be, but the company can't afford to spend too much time on any work until it has proved its popularity. And that can happen only in front of an audience.

The King's Men is the most powerful of several companies of actors operating in the early 17th century. The king's wife, Anne, and their eldest son, Henry, are patrons of their own companies of players. There are also several groups of child actors, such as those at Blackfriars and St Paul's. There is much competition between the companies for good plays. Shakespeare's plays are particularly highly thought of, and the King's Men are determined to be the only company performing them. They are careful not to let Shakespeare's scripts fall into the hands of rivals. Even so, other companies sometimes try to perform their own versions of his plays, usually with incorrect or half-remembered versions of the texts.

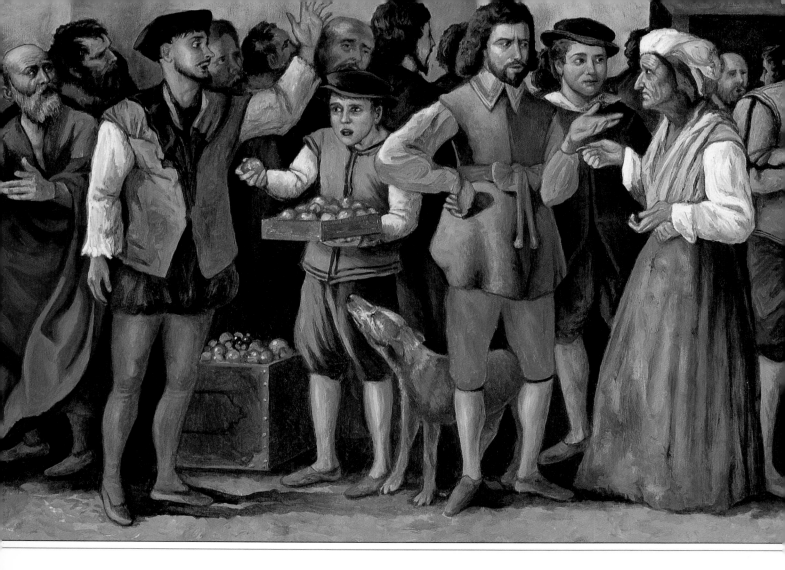

The new play is sure to draw a large audience. It has been well publicised, with playbills stuck on posts all over the city. Shakespeare's name always brings in the crowds.

The company is fortunate that there has not been an outbreak of the plague in the capital – when deaths from the disease reach thirty a week, the City authorities close down all places of public entertainment in an effort to prevent the disease from spreading.

The performance is due to begin at 2 pm. The company flag is flying over the Globe to indicate that a play is being performed today. The poorer folk approach the playhouse via London Bridge. The well-to-do cross the Thames by ferry, some bringing their horses. As they approach the theatre, crowds of boys run up to them offering to look after their animals during the performance for a small fee. Some believe that when Shakespeare first arrived in London he earned his living in this way.

A mass of ordinary people gather in the yard – servants and apprentices, brewers, carters, porters, fishwives, applewives and whores – all jostling for a place with a good view. The crowd is noisy and smelly; the strongest smell is garlic, which many people use as a remedy and as a safeguard against witchcraft. The smell of tobacco smoke occasionally wafts over from the galleries, where fashionable gentlemen sit smoking their long pipes.

Gatherers stand at the doors of the theatre, collecting the entrance fee. Customers pay one penny to enter the yard, which is open to the elements. Those who wish to sit in comfort pay an extra penny to get into the covered galleries, which are sheltered and give a better view. Here they can show off their finery to the rest of the audience. The most expensive seats are in the screened Gentlemen's Rooms or Lords' Rooms near the stage. Before and during the performance hawkers move among the audience selling drinks and snacks.

The First Performance

Three loud knocks signal the start of the performance: the babble of conversation gives way to an expectant hush. Trumpets blare. The noise of thunder rolls down from the Heavens. Three weird female figures appear at the back of the stage, and as they move forwards, one of them begins to speak.

When shall we three meet again?
In thunder, lightning, or in rain...

The play has begun...

. . . Lay on, Macduff;

And damned be him that first cries, 'Hold, enough!'

Macbeth roars out his challenge as trumpets and drums sound from backstage.

The play has reached its climax: a fierce duel between Macbeth and the Scottish lord Macduff, who has come to Scotland with Duncan's son Malcolm and ten thousand English soldiers to overthrow the tyrant.

Swords clashing, Macduff and Macbeth fight their way furiously round the stage, finally disappearing through the curtain at the back. Other actors hack and stab at one another in mock battle. Stage blood seeps crimson onto the boards. The audience love it. Some of the groundlings cheer on Malcolm and his men: women in the galleries utter little screams and cover up their faces with their hands.

Shakespeare has triumphed again.

Macbeth is set in IIth-century Scotland, but the actors speak in their own accents and wear Jacobean clothes. The colour of a player's costume is very important, because it is a sign or symbol to the audience of the nature of the person wearing it. Macbeth is clearly recognisable by his crown and fine scarlet cloak (symbolising blood), worn over a dark costume (symbolising evil). Lady Macbeth's gown of black silk is equally significant. Duncan wears white, indicating purity. His sons are finely attired in silk hose and velvet doublets laced with gold. The witches wear long gowns and caps; the porter wears a grubby leather jerkin. Some of the costumes have been bought second hand, others have been given to the company by wealthy patrons. Together they are worth a fortune and, apart from the theatre itself, are the most valuable property the company owns.

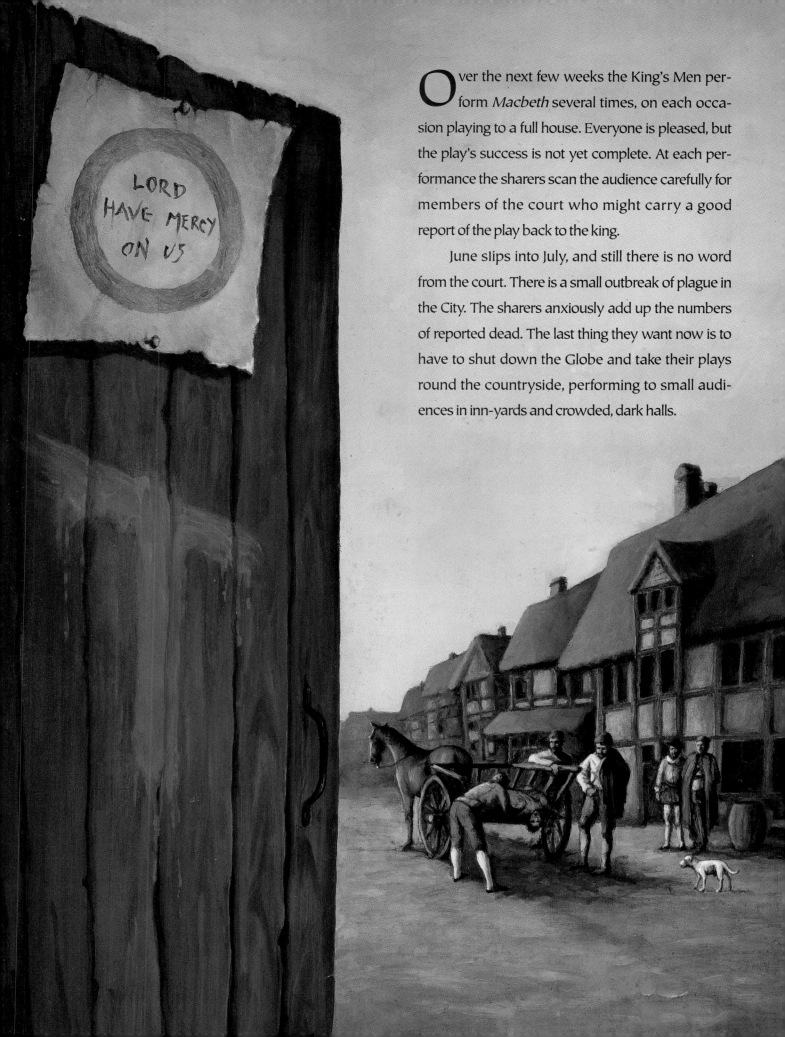

Over the next few weeks the King's Men perform *Macbeth* several times, on each occasion playing to a full house. Everyone is pleased, but the play's success is not yet complete. At each performance the sharers scan the audience carefully for members of the court who might carry a good report of the play back to the king.

June slips into July, and still there is no word from the court. There is a small outbreak of plague in the City. The sharers anxiously add up the numbers of reported dead. The last thing they want now is to have to shut down the Globe and take their plays round the countryside, performing to small audiences in inn-yards and crowded, dark halls.

LORD HAVE MERCY ON US

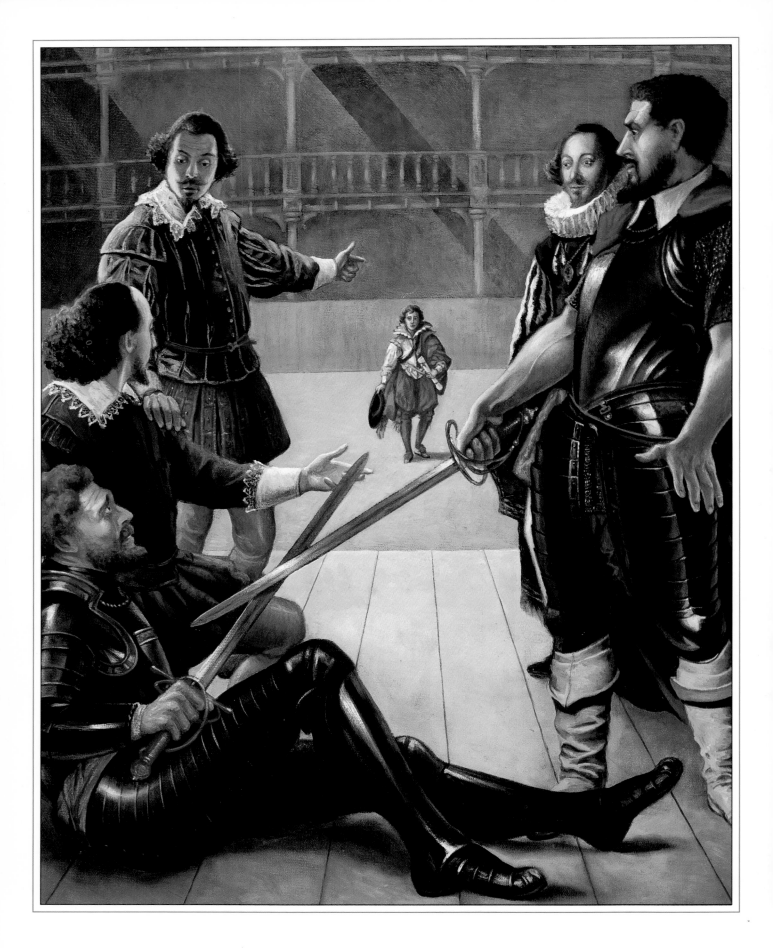

XXX

THIRTY

Then, on the morning of the 1st of August, the long-awaited message finally arrives.

Shakespeare is on stage running through the movements of the fight at the end of *Macbeth*. The previous afternoon, one of the actors dropped his sword in this scene. The weapon flew out of his hand and missed one of the groundlings by inches. Only chance prevented a nasty accident.

One of the actors tugs at Shakespeare's sleeve and points to the yard. A man dressed in the royal livery has slipped in unannounced and is standing watching the rehearsal.

Shakespeare climbs down from the stage and courteously greets the stranger, who hands him a piece of paper. The cast is silent as he stands and reads it. When he has finished, Shakespeare tells the messenger that the company will be delighted to do as the king commands. The messenger smiles, utters a few words and leaves.

As soon as he has gone, Shakespeare waves the paper in the air and calls out the good news to the company: the king has ordered a private showing of *Macbeth* at Hampton Court, before the royal family and the visiting King Christian of Denmark!

Breaking into cheers, the actors and stage hands clasp each other in delight and rush to congratulate Shakespeare. A performance before the king is a great honour. The playwright is clearly thrilled, too. But there is one drawback. The performance is scheduled for the evening of the 7th of August. They have only six days to get everything ready for a court performance.

The King's Men are no strangers at court. Since taking the company under his protection, James I has regularly summoned them to provide entertainment, particularly during the traditional week of Christmas festivities. The payment is £10 a play. This is less than is taken from a full audience at the Globe (which could be £20 or more), but it is useful winter income and is sometimes supplemented with lavish gifts, especially if the king or queen likes the performance.

There are other benefits from court performances besides the money. London's governors have never been keen on theatres. In their eyes, plays rank with bearbaiting and other large-scale entertainments as centres of rowdiness and bad behaviour, drawing young men away from their work in the afternoons. As a result, the governors are always on the lookout for excuses to close the theatres down. Royal approval is a useful shield against such official harassment.

XXXI
THIRTY-ONE

The day following the royal summons, Shakespeare and four of his colleagues take a boat upriver to Hampton Court, to speak with the royal Revels Office. They are told that the Great Hall will be made available to them on the day of the performance, but not before. The Office will provide candles and torches for lighting, and will also help with costumes and material to cover the screen at the end of the hall. The actors have reluctantly decided to cancel their Globe performance on the afternoon of the court appearance, as there will not be enough time to get themselves and their costumes and props from the Globe to Hampton Court for an 8 pm start. This means that they will have the whole day to rehearse *Macbeth* at Hampton Court. As it turns out, much of the day is wasted. Some of the company arrive late,

and the hammering of carpenters putting up temporary seating in the hall makes a mockery of the rehearsal. Nevertheless, by 7 pm, everything is just about ready. The musicians begin to play. Behind the screen the actors make last-minute adjustments to their costumes, check their props and run through their lines. Even the most experienced among them are nervous – a court performance is a tricky undertaking. If it goes wrong or is not well received, the company's reputation will be ruined.

As King of Scotland, James had been the head of what the English saw as a poor third-rate kingdom on the edge of European politics. Before his journey to London in 1603 to claim the English throne, his only trip out of Scotland had been to Denmark to collect his bride, Anne. By 1606 he is rich beyond his wildest dreams. He is ruler of all Britain, and regarded as one of Europe's foremost Protestant monarchs.

The Court Performance

For the past few days King James has been enjoying himself enormously. His brother-in-law, King Christian of Denmark, is on his first state visit to England, and James has had a fine time showing off the wealth of his kingdom.

King Christian is not a difficult man to entertain. As long as there is a bottle of good wine close at hand, he is perfectly happy. Memories of Queen Elizabeth's rather austere court have begun to fade: all is now lavish entertainment and revelry.

The performance of *Macbeth* follows a typically drunken banquet. The first guests wander in from the dining room at about 8.15 pm. Chatting loudly and none too steady on their feet, they take their seats in screened boxes which have been erected in front of the stage. Ten minutes later, the royal family appears. James is leaning on Christian's arm and laughing uproariously. Queen Anne follows behind, accompanied by her ladies-in-waiting and the two royal princes, Henry and Charles. The audience rises in respectful silence.

Shakespeare stands anxiously behind the screen, waiting for a signal from the Master of Revels that the royal party is ready for the performance to begin. Desperately keen that the play is appreciated, he hopes that his flattering references will not be taken amiss. He has deliberately left out of *Macbeth* Holinshed's mention of a Scottish victory over the Danes. But perhaps he has made a mistake in bringing witches onto the stage? And what if James takes offence at Malcolm's needing English help to overcome Macbeth?

He sighs as he watches the witches slip through the doorway onto the brightly lit stage. Whatever second thoughts he might be having, it is too late to change anything now.

XXXV
THIRTY-FIVE

Macbeth

The play begins with three witches on a lonely heath. They are waiting for Macbeth. They set the sinister mood of the whole play with the words:

Fair is foul, and foul is fair.

When the gentle, respected King Duncan appears on stage in the next scene, he learns that Macbeth, Thane (Lord) of Glamis, has won brilliant victories over rebel troops and invading Norwegians. Duncan is overjoyed and decides to give the 'worthy gentle-man' the additional title of Thane of Cawdor.

The scene then shifts back to the witches.

A drum, a drum!
Macbeth doth come.

Caught up in the play, King James leans forward to see Macbeth.

Macbeth enters with his friend Banquo: they are travelling back from the battlefield together. Suddenly, they come across the three weird sisters. The first witch greets Macbeth by his title, Thane of Glamis. But then the second witch greets him as Thane of Cawdor, while the third cries out:

All hail, Macbeth, that shalt be king hereafter!

Macbeth is startled. Are they prophesying that he will be Thane of Cawdor and King of Scotland? Before disappearing, the witches tell Banquo that although he won't be king himself, his descendants will be. At this point the Earl of Ross enters and gives Macbeth the news that Duncan has made him Thane of Cawdor. The first prophecy has come true! The seeds of Macbeth's dark ambition are sown.

When Macbeth arrives home, his wife fans this ambition. She skilfully persuades him to fulfil the second prophecy. King Duncan is due to stay at their castle that night. Macbeth must murder him, she urges, and then seize the throne for himself. After a fierce fight with his conscience, Macbeth gives in. He will kill Duncan as he sleeps. A buzz of excitement runs around the audience.

Even before the murder, Macbeth is deeply troubled. On his way to the king's bedchamber, he imagines that he sees the murder weapon.

Is this a dagger which I see before me …?

It proves to be merely a vision. Later, when he has killed Duncan, he believes he hears a voice calling:

'Sleep no more!
Macbeth doth murder sleep …'

He is so shaken that he forgets part of the plan – to smear Duncan's sleeping servants with blood and leave their daggers in Duncan's room, to make them look guilty of the crime. Lady Macbeth upbraids Macbeth for his weakness. She takes the daggers back to the bedchamber herself.

At this moment, the scene changes. A knocking at the castle gate wakes the porter from his drunken sleep. His clowning helps the audience to relax after the tension of the murder. He imagines himself the keeper of the gates of Hell, welcoming in people who are recognisable to the audience.

But the knocking continues, and when the porter opens the gate, he meets the lords Macduff and Lennox. Macduff has come to wake the king. He discovers Duncan's murder with the cry:

Oh horror, horror, horror!

In the ensuing chaos Duncan's sons, Donalbain and Malcolm, decide to flee abroad. This unwise move gives the impression that they are to blame, and Macbeth is chosen as their father's successor. The witches' second prophecy has come true.

But Macbeth does not rest easy. Remembering the witches' other prophecy, that Banquo's family would one day rule over Scotland, Macbeth hires killers to murder Banquo and his son Fleance. Unlike Duncan, Banquo is killed on stage. The mutilated corpse is left lying in a pool of blood.

To James's delight, his ancestor Fleance manages to escape. One of the murderers observes:

We have lost
Best half of our affair . . .

. . . at which James gives a little cheer. He tries to wake Christian, to tell him why the remark is so apt.

The next scene is a banquet which takes place in Macbeth's palace. Pages bring on a long table and several chairs, and the musicians in the gallery play soothing airs.

Just when all seems to be going well, the murderers enter and tell Macbeth of Banquo's death and Fleance's escape. At the news, the king's anxiety returns. He does his best to appear normal, but all of a sudden a ghastly apparition slides onto the stage from the right-hand door.

It is the ghost of Banquo, his face white and his wounds gaping horribly. The audience gasp in dismay. The ghost sits down at the head of the table, in the place that has been reserved for Macbeth.

At first Macbeth thinks the ghost is some sort of cruel practical joke by his courtiers. When he realises that only he can see the phantom, he screams at it to go away. His dinner guests stare at him in bewildered horror. Lady Macbeth makes excuses for her husband and hurriedly ushers the dinner guests out.

By this time, Macbeth's ruthlessness is becoming clear to everyone. He decides that he may as well give up pretending to be virtuous and continue his campaign of tyranny and slaughter.

> *...I am in blood*
> *Stepped in so far, that, should I wade no more,*
> *Returning were as tedious as go o'er.*
> *Strange things I have in head, that will to hand...*

Macduff is next on his list.

Macbeth visits the witches again, to see if they have any more prophecies. They warn him to beware of Macduff. Then they tell him that no man born of a woman will be able to harm him, and that he will remain king until Birnam Wood comes to Dunsinane Hill, where Macbeth has his castle. 'That will never be,' he says, knowing that these things are impossible.

Finally, he asks whether it is true that Banquo's descendants will be kings of Scotland. By way of reply, the witches show him a procession of eight kings, all of whom look like Banquo. The last holds up a magic mirror to the audience. This is not only a symbol of many more kings in the same line, but also allows King James to see his own reflection. He claps his hands in appreciation and the audience breaks into applause. Behind the screen, Shakespeare smiles to himself.

The bloodshed continues. Macduff flees to join Malcolm in England, leaving behind his wife and children, who are murdered by Macbeth's henchmen. The stabbing of Macduff's little son, played by one of the cast's children, brings a groan of sorrow from the audience.

Safely over the border, Macduff is welcomed by Malcolm, but it is a while before Duncan's son is convinced that Macduff is not Macbeth's spy. The scene is full of wordy argument, and drags on for rather a long time. The audience shuffle their feet and cough. Some of them call for drinks. Shakespeare grows uneasy. In the end, however, after Macduff has been informed of the dreadful fate of his family, Malcolm accepts him. They join forces and prepare to launch their attack.

The pace of the play now picks up rapidly. Short scenes follow each other in quick succession. Macbeth is like a cornered animal. His wife, tormented by the memory of what she has done, walks in her sleep, washing her hands in a vain attempt to rid them of Duncan's blood.

Here's the smell of the blood still. All the perfumes of Arabia will not sweeten this little hand. Oh! oh! oh!

She dies shortly afterwards. In a despairing soliloquy, Macbeth describes life as:

> *...a walking shadow, a poor player*
> *That struts and frets his hour upon the stage*
> *And then is heard no more. It is a tale*
> *Told by an idiot, full of sound and fury,*
> *Signifying nothing.*

As his army marches towards Dunsinane, Malcolm orders his soldiers to cut down branches from Birnam Wood and carry them to cover their advance. Thus one of the witches' prophecies is fulfilled. Battle is joined. In the course of the fight, Macbeth meets Macduff. Macduff was taken from his dead mother's womb by a surgeon, and so was not born of woman – hence the second prophecy is fulfilled. They fight. Macduff slays Macbeth, and presents Malcolm with the tyrant's severed head. The nobles hail Malcolm as king of Scotland. Malcolm thanks his supporters, trumpets sound for the last time, and the play comes to a triumphant end.

Before the final notes have died away, the court breaks into loud applause, led by King James. Even Christian wakes up and joins in. The whole evening has been an unqualified success.

Standing with the other actors at the front of the stage, Shakespeare bows low to the king. He has a broad grin on his face. The performance has confirmed his place as the greatest dramatist of his age.

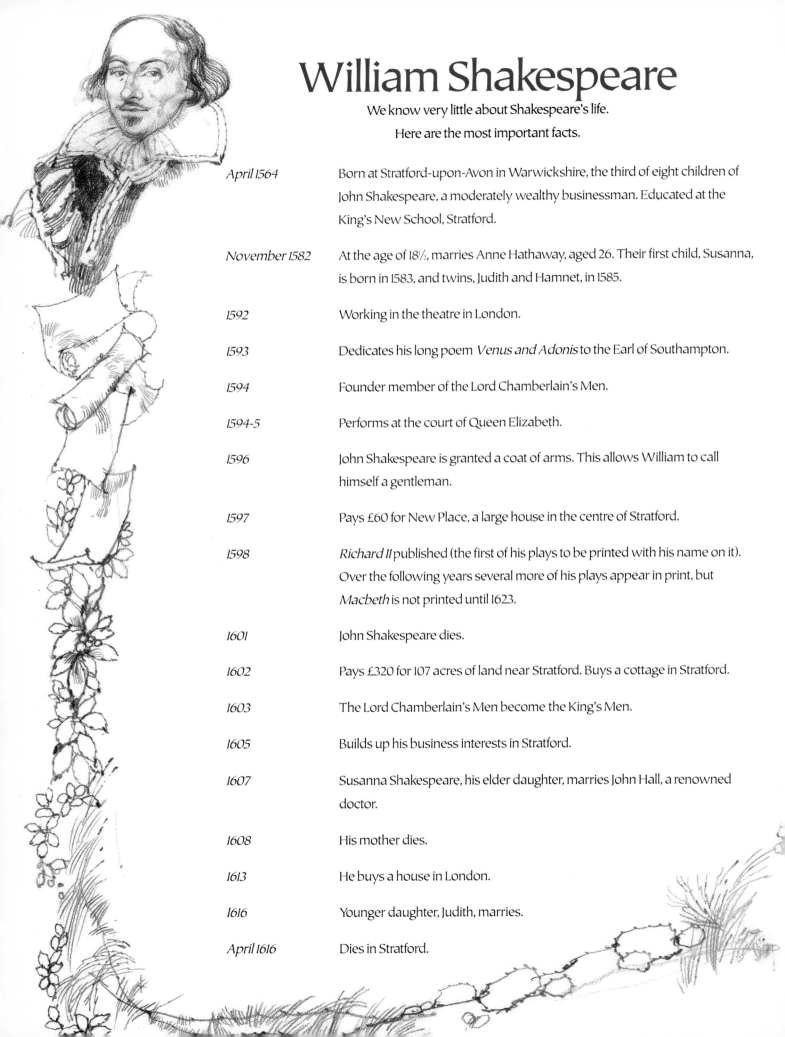

William Shakespeare

We know very little about Shakespeare's life.
Here are the most important facts.

April 1564	Born at Stratford-upon-Avon in Warwickshire, the third of eight children of John Shakespeare, a moderately wealthy businessman. Educated at the King's New School, Stratford.
November 1582	At the age of 18½, marries Anne Hathaway, aged 26. Their first child, Susanna, is born in 1583, and twins, Judith and Hamnet, in 1585.
1592	Working in the theatre in London.
1593	Dedicates his long poem *Venus and Adonis* to the Earl of Southampton.
1594	Founder member of the Lord Chamberlain's Men.
1594-5	Performs at the court of Queen Elizabeth.
1596	John Shakespeare is granted a coat of arms. This allows William to call himself a gentleman.
1597	Pays £60 for New Place, a large house in the centre of Stratford.
1598	*Richard II* published (the first of his plays to be printed with his name on it). Over the following years several more of his plays appear in print, but *Macbeth* is not printed until 1623.
1601	John Shakespeare dies.
1602	Pays £320 for 107 acres of land near Stratford. Buys a cottage in Stratford.
1603	The Lord Chamberlain's Men become the King's Men.
1605	Builds up his business interests in Stratford.
1607	Susanna Shakespeare, his elder daughter, marries John Hall, a renowned doctor.
1608	His mother dies.
1613	He buys a house in London.
1616	Younger daughter, Judith, marries.
April 1616	Dies in Stratford.

The Play

Ever since its first performance, *Macbeth* has remained one of Shakespeare's most popular plays. It is still given hundreds of performances all over the world every year. It has been translated into dozens of languages and filmed several times. Few great stage actors and actresses regard their careers as complete until they have played either Macbeth or Lady Macbeth.

Apart from the fascinating characters of the two leading roles, the play's chief attraction is its wonderful poetry. Scarcely a word is wasted, and vivid images tumble after each other in a stream of colour and ideas. The language is so dense, however, that when you first read it, you may not find it easy to understand.

There are one or two other problems for a modern audience. For example, we find it difficult to take the witches seriously. And as *Macbeth* was not printed until nearly 20 years after it had been written, we cannot be sure that the version we have is what Shakespeare wrote. Scholars argue endlessly about what is and what is not the correct text.

In the theatre *Macbeth* has an unlucky reputation. Perhaps because it is concerned so closely with evil, actors do not like to mention the name of the play or quote from it, except on stage. They call it 'The Scottish Play', and perform strange rituals if they speak a line from it by mistake!

Nevertheless, despite the worries of actors and the squabbles of scholars, *Macbeth* remains one of the finest plays in our language.

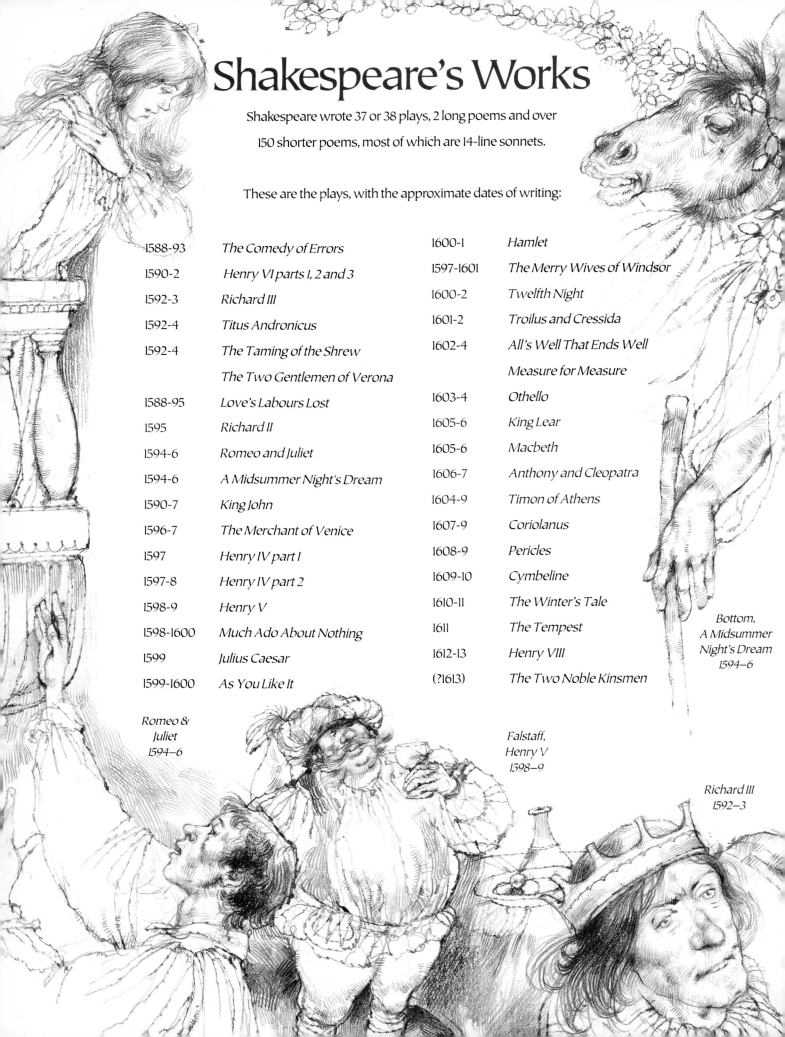

Shakespeare's Works

Shakespeare wrote 37 or 38 plays, 2 long poems and over
150 shorter poems, most of which are 14-line sonnets.

These are the plays, with the approximate dates of writing:

1588-93	*The Comedy of Errors*		1600-1	*Hamlet*
1590-2	*Henry VI parts 1, 2 and 3*		1597-1601	*The Merry Wives of Windsor*
1592-3	*Richard III*		1600-2	*Twelfth Night*
1592-4	*Titus Andronicus*		1601-2	*Troilus and Cressida*
1592-4	*The Taming of the Shrew*		1602-4	*All's Well That Ends Well*
	The Two Gentlemen of Verona			*Measure for Measure*
1588-95	*Love's Labours Lost*		1603-4	*Othello*
1595	*Richard II*		1605-6	*King Lear*
1594-6	*Romeo and Juliet*		1605-6	*Macbeth*
1594-6	*A Midsummer Night's Dream*		1606-7	*Anthony and Cleopatra*
1590-7	*King John*		1604-9	*Timon of Athens*
1596-7	*The Merchant of Venice*		1607-9	*Coriolanus*
1597	*Henry IV part 1*		1608-9	*Pericles*
1597-8	*Henry IV part 2*		1609-10	*Cymbeline*
1598-9	*Henry V*		1610-11	*The Winter's Tale*
1598-1600	*Much Ado About Nothing*		1611	*The Tempest*
1599	*Julius Caesar*		1612-13	*Henry VIII*
1599-1600	*As You Like It*		(?1613)	*The Two Noble Kinsmen*

*Romeo &
Juliet
1594–6*

*Falstaff,
Henry V
1598–9*

*Bottom,
A Midsummer
Night's Dream
1594–6*

*Richard III
1592–3*

Index

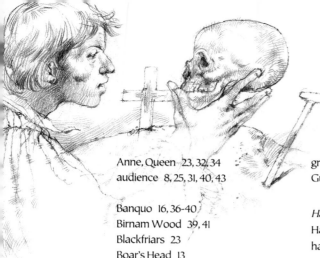

Hamlet
1600–1

Julius Caesar
1599

Further Reading

There are many modern editions of *Macbeth*, most of which include helpful notes on the text and staging of the play. Other scholarly works include:

Bernard Beckerman, *Shakespeare at the Globe 1599-1609*, New York, 1962.

Herbert Berry, *Shakespeare's Playhouses*, New York, 1987.

R.A. Foakes, *Illustrations of the London Stage*, London, 1985.

Andrew Gurr, *The Shakespearean Stage 1574-1642* (Third Edition), Cambridge, 1992.

Andrew Gurr, *Playgoing in Shakespeare's London*, Cambridge, 1987.

F.E. Halliday, *A Shakespeare Companion 1564-1964*, Harmondsworth, 1964.

G.B. Harrison, *Introducing Shakespeare* (Third Edition), Harmondsworth, 1966.

Samuel Schoenbaum, *William Shakespeare. A Compact Documentary Life*, Oxford, 1977.